ALL THINGS POLAR BEARS FOR KIDS

FILLED WITH PLENTY OF FACTS, PHOTOS, AND FUN TO LEARN ALL ABOUT POLAR BEARS

ANIMAL READS

WWW.ANIMALREADS.COM

THIS BOOK BELONGS TO...

_____

_____

WWW.ANIMALREADS.COM

CONTENTS

A Polar Bear Guide For Young Explorers	1
Meet the Polar Bear	7
Polar Bear Habitat	23
Polar Bear Diet	29
Polar Bear Behavior	37
Polar Bear Life Cycle	45
Amazing Polar Bear Facts!	53
Polar Bear Conservation	59
You Polar Bear Expert You!	65
Thank You!	71

A POLAR BEAR GUIDE FOR YOUNG EXPLORERS

You might have never been to the Arctic, but that's no reason not to get to know one of the Arctic's best-loved residents —**the polar bear.** Throughout these pages, we'll slide, swim, and laugh our way through some amazing facts about these *icy cool* creatures!

The Arctic is a tough place to live, but for polar bears, it's home. If you lived in such a snowy place, you'd need a lot of help to stay warm and survive, but not polar bears!

These cuddly-looking creatures are nicknamed the "***Kings & Queens of the Arctic***," and they are perfectly suited for their icy habitat. Just look at some of the "*snow gear*" they have:

- Big paws to help them walk on snow and ice!
- Thick double-coated fur and blubber to keep them warm in freezing temps!
- An amazing sense of smell to help them find food in the snow!
- A bright white color to help them blend in with their snowy surroundings!

Are you ready to explore the Arctic world of these furry giants? **There is so much to discover!** Remember, every page you turn, every picture you see, and every fact you learn brings you one step closer to becoming a Polar Bear Expert! *Now, isn't that exciting?*

Alrighty then! Let's put on our snow goggles, hop onto our sleds, and glide into the next chapter! **The polar bears are waiting!**

MEET THE POLAR BEAR
FURRY ICE GIANTS

So, let's get to know our friends a little bit better, and that all starts with how they are classified. Polar bears are **mammals**, just like us humans! They have fur, give birth to live cubs, and even produce milk for their young. So we can call them our "furry cousins" from the icy Arctic!

Polar bears are also **carnivores**, which means they eat meat. They are actually the largest land carnivores on Earth! Males can grow as big as 10 feet long and weigh up to 1,600 pounds. Females are slightly smaller but still massive, coming in at around 8 feet long and up to 1,100 pounds.

Can you imagine meeting a bear that big? To help you picture this, imagine a bear, like a refrigerator, that's as tall as your ceiling and as wide as your front door! **That's one giant bear!**

Polar bears belong to a big family called *Ursidae* in the scientific world. This family consists of other bear species like the cuddly, bamboo-eating pandas and the impressive grizzly bears. The scientific world gave polar bears the unique name *Ursus maritimus*, which sounds very fancy, but it just means "**sea bear.**" They get this name because polar bears spend most of their time swimming and fishing in icy waters. In fact, even though polar bears also spend time on land, they are actually classified as **marine mammals**, just like dolphins, whales, and seals!

ANATOMY OF A POLAR BEAR

Polar bears have lived in icy conditions for a long time, and they show it! They are perfectly suited to this chilly environment. Let's take a closer look at each part of these giant bears and how they are a perfect match for life in the Arctic.

FUR

One of the most important parts of a polar bear is its coat. No animal lives long in the Arctic without some serious way to keep warm, and polar bears are no different. A polar bear's first secret to warmth is in their skin.

Even though a polar bear looks white as snow, their skin is actually black! This dark skin helps them soak up warmth from the sun.

On top of their skin, a polar bear doesn't just have one layer of fur, but two! On the bottom is a dense layer of insulating underfur (*kind of like when you put on long underwear during winter to keep warm*). Over that, they have an outer layer of guard hairs. These hairs are not actually white but *transparent*, which makes them look white because they reflect the light. This fur keeps them warm and also provides camouflage in a snowy environment.

PAWS

To pad about on snow all day, a polar bear has to have specially-built paws. These giant paws are about 12 inches wide and act like snowshoes, allowing them to walk on soft ice and snow without falling through.

Since they spend most of their time on ice or swimming in water, you might wonder how they manage to not slip and slide all over the place. The bottoms of their feet have paw pads, which are covered in tiny bumps called *papillae*. These papillae work almost like suction cups and help polar bears grip the ice when they're walking or dashing after a tasty meal. To help keep their feet warm and cozy, polar bear paws are also covered in coarse fur to keep the chills away.

Polar bears' front paws are especially helpful when they swim. They use their large feet to paddle in the icy waters, using them like oars while their back legs steer.

SENSE OF SMELL AND TEETH

Polar bears have an incredible sense of smell. In fact, their noses are so good at finding food that they can sniff out a seal from miles away—even when that seal is hidden under ice. Imagine if you had a super powerful nose like that. You'd be able to find your favorite snack anywhere in the house!

Now, if you think your teeth are strong, polar bears put you to shame with their impressive chompers. Their mouths are filled with 42 powerful teeth designed to crush and chew through thick ice, blubber, and tough bones.

While blubber and bones may not be your favorite thing to eat, it's a tasty meal for polar bears! We will explore more of their diets and how they eat in just a couple of pages, but first, what's behind these bears?

A short ...

TAIL

Even though a polar bear's tiny tail may not seem impressive, it actually plays a big role. Like most bears, polar bears have short and stubby tails. *So, what kind of job could a tail like that have?* A polar bear's tail actually has an important role in helping the bear stay warm.

Have you ever tried to sleep when it was super cold out? We bet your face felt frozen! You probably pulled your blankets up to keep your face warm, right? **Polar bears aren't that different.** When it gets *REALLY* cold outside, a polar bear will curl up into a ball, making it look like a giant, furry snowball. **It will tuck its nose under its tail, creating a little air pocket that traps warm air around its face.** This allows the bear to sleep and not wake up with ice all over its face!

A SWIMMER'S BODY

Polar bears may not look like they have the build of an Olympic swimmer, but they're actually amazing in the water! *How do they do it?* Their bodies are perfectly designed for life in the chilly Arctic waters.

Remember how you learned that polar bears have fur with two layers? Here is where those layers come in extra handy. The outer layer, with its long hairs, is actually waterproof. This way, the polar bear can swim and not even feel wet because their soft inner layer of hair stays dry.

This layer also traps in their body heat so they don't get cold. Pretty cool, huh?

Polar bears get to use their big feet best when swimming. They have huge paws that work like built-in flippers in the water. And when we say "big," we mean it! Their paws are as big as dinner plates! These large feet make it easy for polar bears to paddle through the water at top speeds.

A polar bear's large, chubby body also comes in handy as they swim. *Have you ever noticed how some swimming animals have sleek bodies, like a dolphin, but other animals, like a walrus, seem kinda chubby?*

Animals that live in chilly water have to have some way to stay warm, and a big way they keep warm is through the use of fat layers called "*blubber*." Polar bears also have a "blubber layer" that helps them stay warm and store energy while swimming long distances. This blubber layer can also be used by their bodies and converted into energy if they need it.

You know how swimmers wear goggles to see underwater? Well, polar bears don't need them! They have something even better: a special membrane that covers their eyes while swimming. This membrane helps them to see clearly without getting water in their eyes. They basically have their own **built-in** goggles.

Polar bears may not look like athletic Olympic swimmers, but they are big, furry swimming machines! Few other animals are built for water like they are, with their waterproof fur, paddle-like paws, a built-in blubber layer, and built-in water goggles. They also have amazing endurance! Polar bears can swim for miles and miles without ever getting tired, all while staying warm and dry in the icy Arctic waters. We'd like to see an Olympic swimmer try to compete with that!

WHY DO POLAR BEARS HAVE THICK COATS?

FUR protection!

POLAR BEAR HABITAT
FROSTY HOMES AND ICY HANGOUTS

P olar bears live in the chilly Arctic region. Their habitat mainly consists of sea ice, which is like a giant frozen blanket covering the ocean. Polar bears spend most of their time on this icy surface, as it helps them catch their favorite meal—seals! They rely on the sea ice to travel, hunt, and sometimes even build their cozy dens there.

Polar bears inhabit the icy realms of the Arctic Circle. They call places like Canada, Russia, Greenland, Norway, and Alaska their frosty home. The Arctic region isn't an easy neighborhood to live in for most creatures, but as we've learned, polar bears are experts at adapting to their frosty surroundings.

But what about baby polar bears? How do they survive such a cold place? Just like other mother bears, polar bears like to build dens when they are expecting to give birth to baby cubs.

You might be wondering how anyone could build a den out of ice? Polar bears instinctually know how to dig snug snow caves called "maternity dens." These cozy spots become the perfect nurseries for the moms and their cubs.

Finding the perfect place for a den requires a few considerations. First of all, momma bears like to have their maternity dens in snowdrifts. You see, the snow acts like a blanket that keeps them warm and free from chilly winds.

When looking where to build, location, location, location is everything, even for polar bears! A momma bear looks for a spot where the snowpack is just right for digging a den. *Too shallow, and the mama won't have enough room to wiggle around inside it. Too deep, and the mom and babies might get lost in a snow maze!*

Once the mama bear has found the best spot for her den, she gets to digging and creates a cozy den to use for welcoming her new cubs into the world.

POLAR BEAR DIET

It takes a lot of food to fuel an animal as big as a bear, especially a polar bear! *But what food is available in a frozen place like the Arctic?* Polar bears are carnivores, and it's a good thing, too, since not much can grow there. Carnivores are animals that only eat meat, like lions, great white sharks, and wolves. For the most part, they don't eat any fruits, vegetables, or anything else, just meat.

It may not seem tasty to you, but seals are a polar bear's favorite food. Seals provide a lot of things a polar bear needs, such as essential nutrients and blubber.

Polar bears need to eat about 4.4 to 5.5 pounds of pure blubber each day. That might not sound like a lot, but a little pure fat goes a long way! The blubber gives them energy to keep hunting and exploring the icy tundra they call home. But blubber isn't all they eat; they also eat meat.

You may be wondering just how much a polar bear eats in one meal? If there was an eating contest in the Arctic, they just might win! Polar bears can eat a whopping 150-200 pounds of food in just one meal! Pretty amazing!

While they mostly feast on seals, they might also munch on little fish, birds, or even kelp. Also, when given the chance, polar bears will hunt and eat walruses, beluga whales, and the occasional reindeer! During times when there isn't much food available, they will chow down on whatever they can get.

Now you might be thinking, *"If they need to eat so much, they must have to eat all the time!"* But that's not entirely true. Polar bears have a unique way of eating, called **_feasting and fasting_**. This means they have big meals, like their 200-pound seal special, and then they don't eat much at all for a while. They can even go without food for months during the lean times when food is scarce.

Even though it sounds strange, this way of eating actually works for polar bears. They're built for this feast and famine lifestyle. Their bodies can store lots of fat to keep them going during those fasting times when food is hard to come by.

HUNTING TECHNIQUES

Since there aren't many carnivore cafes in the Arctic, polar bears have to catch all their own food. Thankfully, they are good hunters and have developed some pretty smart strategies when it comes to finding a tasty seal meal.

To catch a seal, polar bears use a method called "*still-hunting.*" **It takes a lot of patience!**

To do this, a polar bear finds a breathing hole in the ice. Seals can stay underwater for a long time, but eventually, they need to come up for air. Polar bears know this and wait near breathing holes in the ice. When a seal comes up for air, the polar bear jumps into action and grabs it. They snatch up the seal with their powerful paws and pull them right out of the water.

Of course, polar bears don't just stick to hunting on the ice. Since they are great swimmers, they often hop in to hunt for seals and fish underwater as well.

WHY ARE POLAR BEARS POPULAR AT PARTIES?

Because they know how to break the ice!

POLAR BEAR BEHAVIOR
BEAR CHIT-CHAT AND SOCIALIZING SECRETS!

When polar bears want to chat with one another, they don't use text messages or apps like we do – instead, they rely on their own unique language. This includes a variety of vocalizations, body language, and even some friendly wrestling. Polar bears exchange signals to communicate with each other. If you ever see two polar bears playing together, remember that it's not just a game – they're actually having a conversation!

But do polar bears socialize like we do? Do they have friends? Polar bears are alone a lot, but they do make friends, too. A lot depends on the season. During the ice-free season, polar bears are concentrated on land and have to share a smaller space with each other. This allows them to interact and build relationships with each other. But even though they like to get together sometimes, when it's time to hunt or take care of their cubs, polar bears prefer to be alone.

COMMUNICATION DEEP DIVE

Polar bears have a whole range of vocalizations, from growls and chuffs to moans and snorts. These sounds mean different things, like "*Please leave me alone!*" or "*Hey, you're pretty cool!*" It's not too different from when you talk to your friends but with more, well, bear noises!

For example, a mama bear might use a chuff to tell her cubs, "Come here, little ones!" And if one of them wanders too far? She'll let out a stern growl to say, "Get back here now!"

If two bears meet each other, they might sniff their noses and make chuffing sounds. It's like their version of a handshake and small talk!

Polar bears don't just talk with their voices, though. Like most animals, they use lots of body language, too! For instance, if a polar bear feels that another bear is too close, it might stand up tall and puff out its chest. This is its way of saying, "I'm big and strong, so don't mess with me!"

If a bear wants to play, it might wag its head and shimmy about, looking like it's ready to dance! This invites other bears to join in the fun.

Polar bears also have another way to communicate: *through using smells and scents*. A polar bear might rub up against the snow or ice, leaving a trail of its unique scent behind. When other bears come along, they can smell the snow and know who else has been there. It's like their version of signing their name or leaving a note that says, "*Burrrnny was here!*"

Marking areas with their scent helps them find friends and sometimes even a potential mate! When a female polar bear is ready to have a family, she'll leave a special smell in her tracks that a male polar bear can sniff out. Once he tracks her down, they can mate, and the female can then go off to build a den and have her cubs.

LIFE IS EASIER WHEN YOU **CHILL** OUT!

POLAR BEAR LIFE CYCLE
FROM CUBS TO ADULTHOOD

It's hard to imagine polar bears were ever tiny, but even the largest snowy giant started life as a small cub.

We learned earlier that when momma polar bears are pregnant and close to giving birth, they look for the perfect place to dig a den. This den, dug into the snow and ice, will be where she welcomes her litter of polar bear babies to the world.

Birthing season is typically in the winter months, between November and February. Baby polar bears are called "cubs." They're born very tiny, weighing as little as one pound! Polar bear moms usually give birth to one to three cubs at a time, but two cubs are the most common litter size. They are born with their eyes closed, and a newborn cub can fit in your hands! Once born, the tiny cubs snuggle up with their mom to nurse and stay in the den during the freezing winter.

Inside the den, the temperature stays comfortably above freezing, perfect for mama bears and their newborns. They spend the entire winter curled up and cozy, waiting for the world outside to warm up. This time in the den typically takes several months. At the end of this time, the mother and her cubs will emerge in the springtime. The cubs have opened their eyes and grown quite a bit by then.

It's an important time for the cubs as it's the first time they go out into their icy habitat and learn all of the ropes. They are usually super wobbly and have so much to learn. The sibling bond is very special since cubs learn a lot from each other. It's helpful to cubs to have a wrestling and chasing partner in the snow, and it helps them build a strong foundation for life in their frosty habitat.

Momma bears do an excellent job of teaching their cubs how to survive in the icy wilderness. They teach their cubs the tricks of the trade, like hunting seals, swimming, and how to walk and not slip on the ice! During this time, the polar bear cubs slowly stop drinking their mothers' milk and start to wean. They now begin to get nutrients from meat, which their mother hunts for them.

As the cubs grow older, they turn into sub-adult polar bears, kind of like teenagers. They're still young and curious but a bit too big to be called cubs. During this time, polar bears practice their hunting skills and explore new territories.

Around the age of 2 or 3, sub-adult polar bears become strong and independent and are ready to face the world on their own.

When female polar bears are about 4 to 5 years old, they can start the cycle over again and begin a family of their own. Males take a bit longer to mature, and some are ready to mate at 6 years old. However, most males take even longer than this and typically mate when they are 8 to 10 years old or older.

The lifespan of polar bears in the wild is usually between 20 to 30 years, although some polar bears have been known to live into their mid-30s.

In captivity, polar bears can live even longer, with some living into their 40s. However, just like how we need to eat well and exercise to stay healthy, polar bears need a healthy environment to live a long life.

Unfortunately, things like climate change and hunting can make it harder for polar bears to survive and live as long as they should.

AMAZING POLAR BEAR FACTS!

You've already learned a lot about polar bears, but take a look at some of these fun facts. We bet even your parents don't know some of these cool trivia tidbits!

UNEXPECTED BEHAVIORS

Let's start with something that might make you giggle—polar bears don't just live in the snow, they play in it too! That's right, these giant fluffballs enjoy sliding down icy hills, rolling around in the snow (*kind of like making snow angels*), and just having a jolly old time. They also like taking long naps in the snow, just like how we enjoy cozying up in our warm beds for a good snooze.

AMUSING ADAPTATIONS

Polar bears have an amazing sense of smell. In fact, it's so good polar bears can smell seals up to a mile away! Imagine being able to sniff out your favorite foods from that far away. You might never lose your lunchbox again!

CURIOUS POLAR BEAR HYGIENE

Did you know that polar bears actually keep themselves clean? After a meal, polar bears love to rub themselves against the snow or ice to clean their fur. They do this because clean fur helps them stay warm in the cold Arctic climate. It's kind of like how we brush our teeth and take showers to stay clean and healthy!

MIGRATION PATTERNS

You may have heard that some animals, like birds, migrate long distances to find warmer weather or better food sources. Well, polar bears have their own interesting migration patterns too! Polar bears usually don't travel too far. Still, they do follow the movement of sea ice, which is their primary hunting ground.

Now, imagine a polar bear walking on a treadmill—that's kind of what it's like when they follow the sea ice! As sea ice moves and changes with the seasons, polar bears go along for the ride. They might walk hundreds of miles just to stay in the same place!

THANK YOU

SNOW

MUCH!

POLAR BEAR CONSERVATION

Sadly, polar bears as a species are in some trouble. They are currently listed as an *endangered species*. This means there aren't as many of them as there once were, and their numbers keep getting smaller and smaller.

So, what is going on? Well, as you learned, our furry friends live in the Arctic, which is like a giant freezer, perfect for keeping them cool. But there's a problem—the "*giant freezer*" is slowly turning into a "*giant refrigerator.*" Climate change is causing the sea ice to melt, which means polar bears have less space to roam and live.

To make matters worse, when the ice melts, polar bears have to swim longer distances to find food, making them very tired. And less ice means fewer spots for them to rest and raise their cubs.

But fear not, young polar bear pals! We can help our friends by joining the battle against climate change. Simple actions to not waste energy (like switching off the lights when you leave a room), using energy-efficient light bulbs, and riding bicycles instead of cars whenever possible can make a difference. It's time for us to step up and be heroes for our furry friends in the Arctic!

You can also lend a helping paw by supporting groups working hard to protect polar bears. Polar Bears International and The World Wildlife Fund (WWF) focus on research, education, and action to conserve these fuzzy giants and their habitat.

YOU POLAR BEAR EXPERT YOU!

Can you believe we've reached the end of our frosty adventure? We bet your brains are bursting with all the cool stuff we've learned about polar bears!

Remember their fancy name? That's right! **Ursus maritimus**, or "sea bear". And boy is that an appropriate name! They can swim for miles and miles, just like fish. They're just much fluffier and have big, round noses. We also talked about where these frosty fellows live, their cozy fur coats, and we can't forget about their favorite foods - seals and fish. Plus, we learned how polar bears grow up, starting as tiny cubs and growing into big, strong bears.

Wow, what a journey! Give yourselves a big round of applause! You're now officially Polar Bear Experts! How cool is that?

Remember to share all these amazing facts with your friends and family. Who knows? You might inspire them to become Polar Bear Experts too!

Remember that even though we've come to the end of this book, your journey as a Polar Bear Expert is just beginning. There are always more fun facts to discover and more ways to help protect our frosty friends and their icy homes. Polar bears everywhere deserve our help. Let's work together to keep our planet a place where all animals can live and thrive for years to come!

So keep exploring, keep learning, and definitely keep having fun! Because every great explorer knows that learning is the greatest adventure of all!

Thank you for joining us on this extraordinary Arctic adventure. Until our next frosty journey together, stay cool!

BEAR WITH ME!

THANK YOU!

Thank you for reading this book and for allowing us to share our love for polar bears with you!

If you've enjoyed this book, please let us know by leaving a rating and a brief review wherever you made your purchase! This helps us spread the word to other readers!

Thank you for your time, and have an awesome day!

For more information, please visit:

www.animalreads.com

WHAT'S A POLAR BEAR'S FAVORITE MEAL?

ICEBERG-ers!

© Copyright 2023 - All rights reserved Admore Publishing

ISBN: 978-3-96772-170-6

ISBN: 978-3-96772-171-3

ISBN: 978-3-96772-172-0

Animal Reads at www.animalreads.com

The content contained within this book may not be reproduced, duplicated or transmitted without direct written permission from the author or the publisher.

Under no circumstances will any blame or legal responsibility be held against the publisher, or author, for any damages, reparation, or monetary loss due to the information contained within this book. Either directly or indirectly.

Published by Admore Publishing: Gotenstraße, Berlin, Germany

www.admorepublishing.com

www.ingramcontent.com/pod-product-compliance
Lightning Source LLC
LaVergne TN
LVHW020142080526
838202LV00048B/3988